Trace & Write
Alphabets and Numbers for Beginning Writers

Preschool | Kindergarten | 1st Grade

Smart Kidz College
978-1511801263

Trace the letter "A"

Trace the letter "A"

Practice writing the letter "A"

Practice writing the letter "A"

A

O

A

O

A

O

Trace the letter "B"

B B B B B B

b b b b b b b

B B B B B B

b b b b b b b

B B B B B

b b b b b b b

Trace the letter "B"

B B B B B B

b b b b b b b

B B B B B B

b b b b b b b

B B B B B B

b b b b b b b

Practice writing the letter "B"

B

b

B

b

B

b

Practice writing the letter "B"

B

b

B

b

B

b

Trace the letter "C"

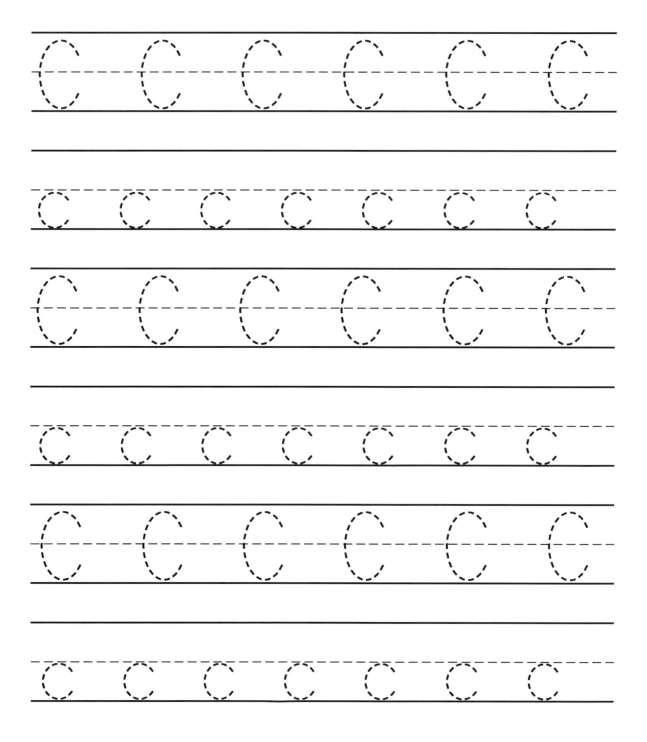

Trace the letter "C"

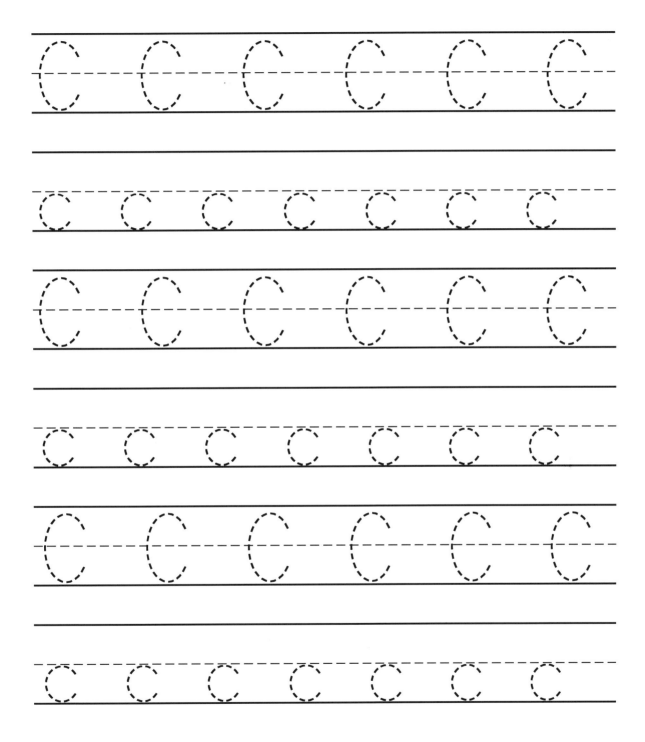

Practice writing the letter "C"

Practice writing the letter "C"

C

C

C

C

C

C

Trace the letter "D"

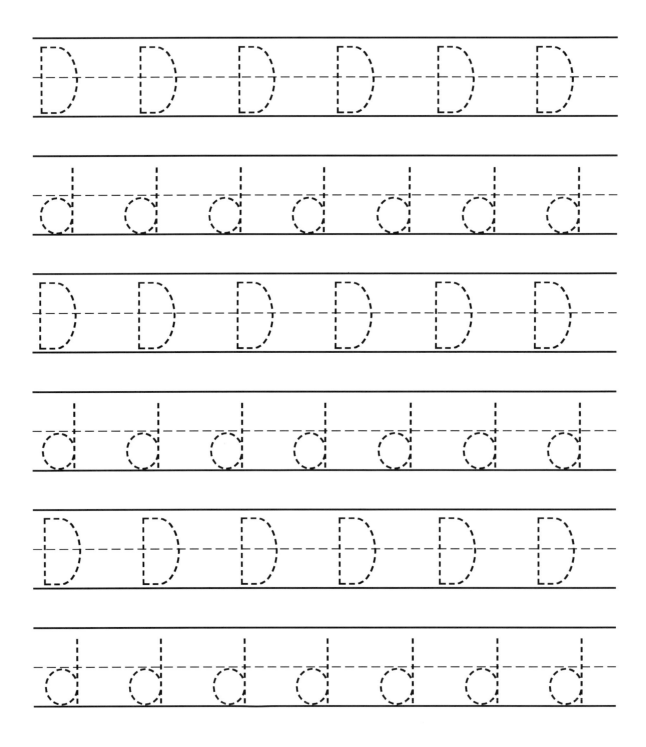

Trace the letter "D"

D D D D D D

d d d d d d d

D D D D D D

d d d d d d d

D D D D D D

d d d d d d d

Practice writing the letter "D"

D -

d -

D -

d -

D -

d -

Practice writing the letter "D"

D

d

D

d

D

d

Trace the letter "E"

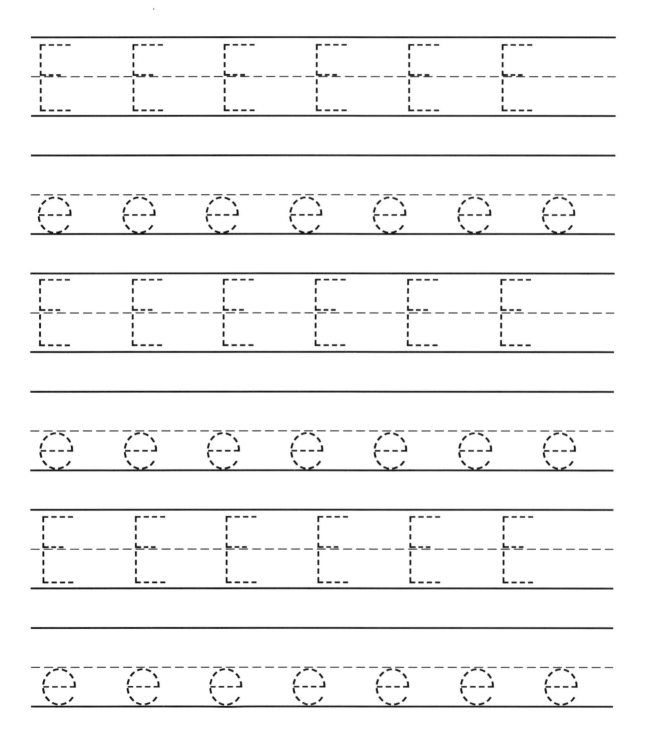

Trace the letter "E"

Practice writing the letter "E"

Practice writing the letter "E"

Trace the letter "F"

Trace the letter "F"

Practice writing the letter "F"

Practice writing the letter "F"

Trace the letter "G"

Trace the letter "G"

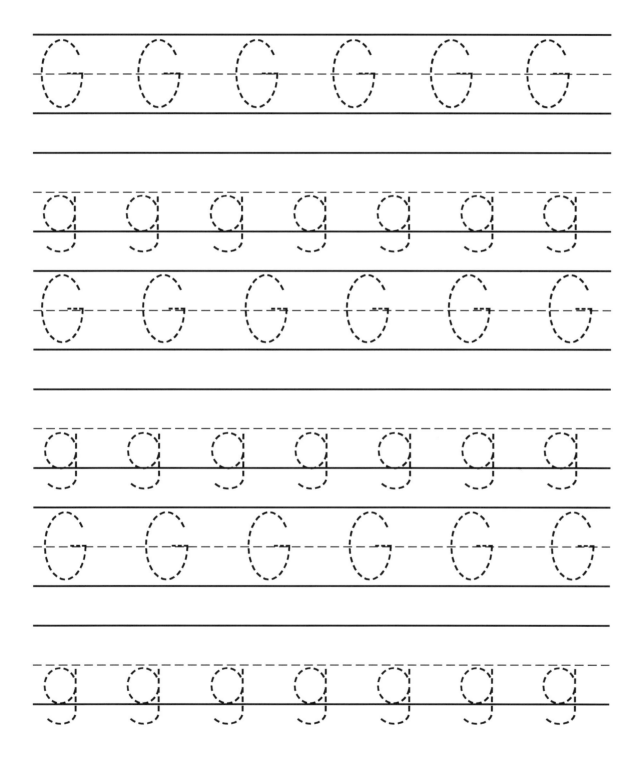

Practice writing the letter "G"

Practice writing the letter "G"

Trace the letter "H"

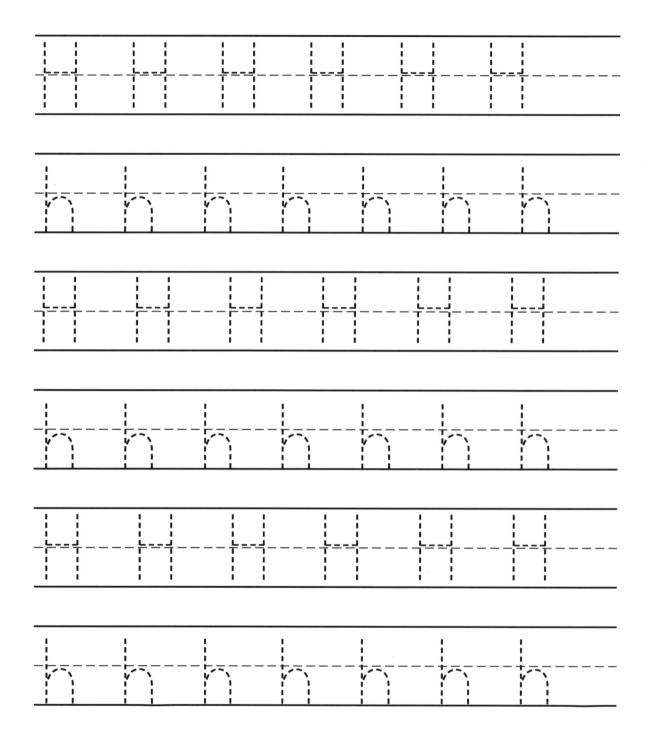

Trace the letter "H"

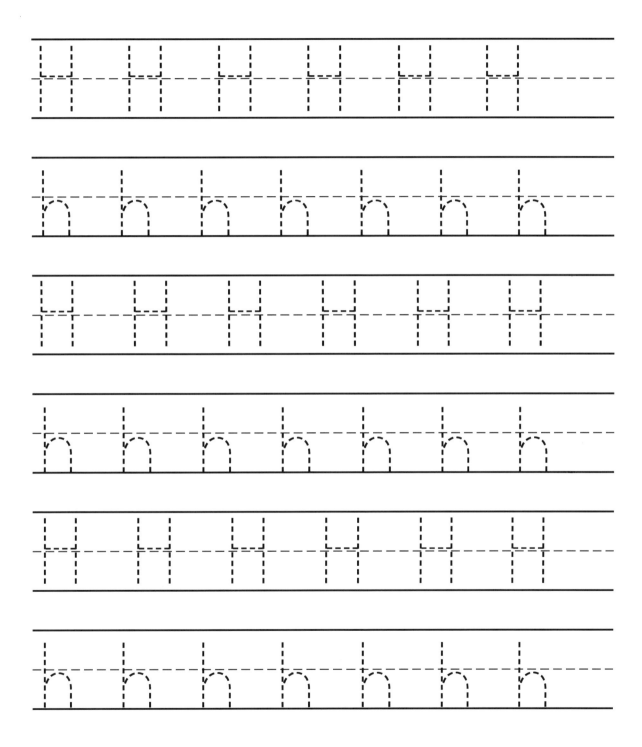

Practice writing the letter "H"

Practice writing the letter "H"

Trace the letter "I"

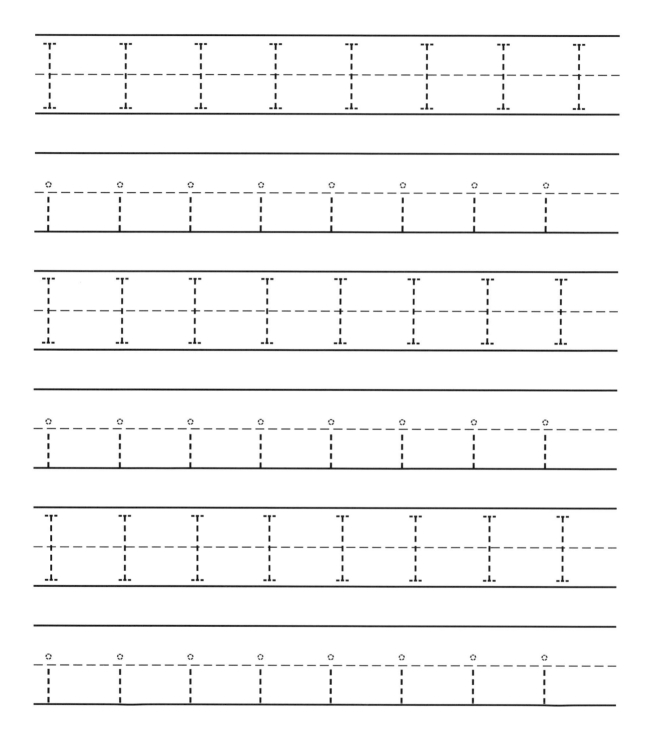

Trace the letter "I"

Practice writing the letter "I"

Practice writing the letter "I"

Trace the letter "J"

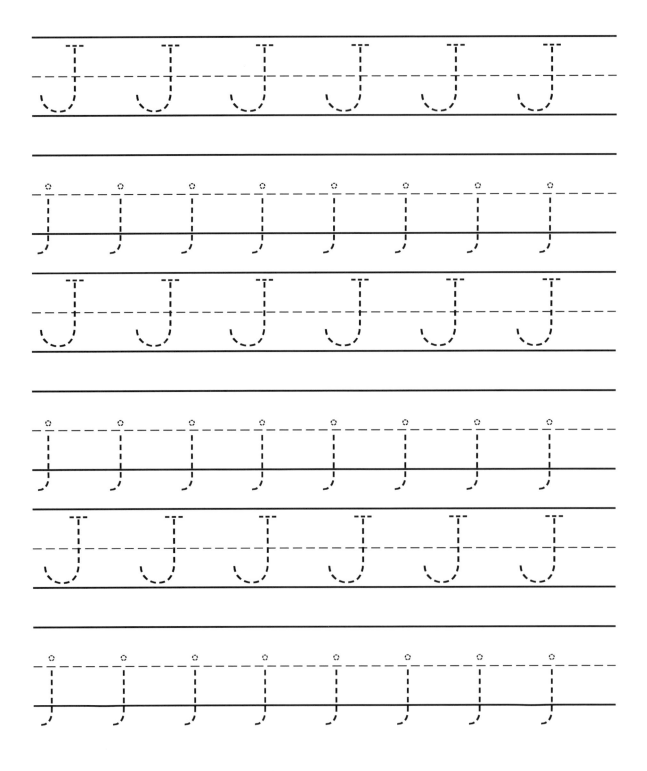

Trace the letter "J"

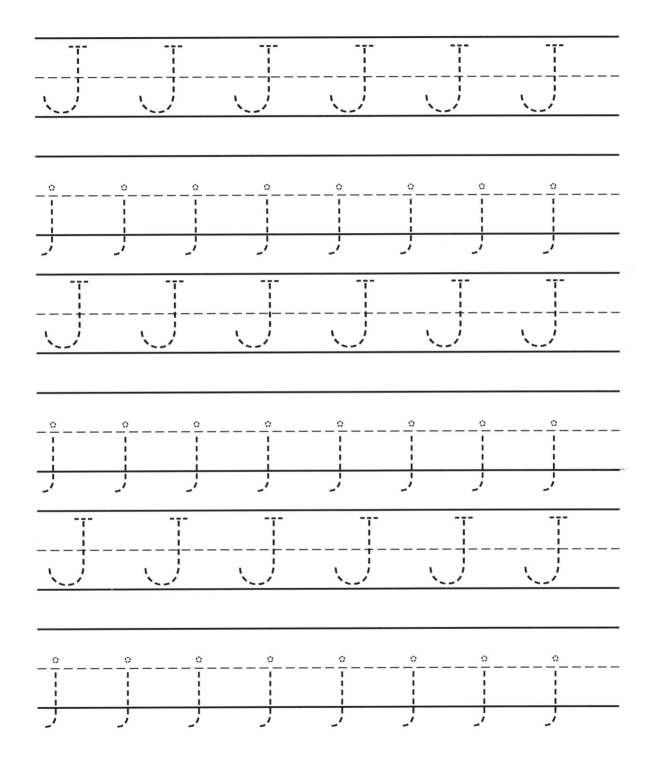

Practice writing the letter "J"

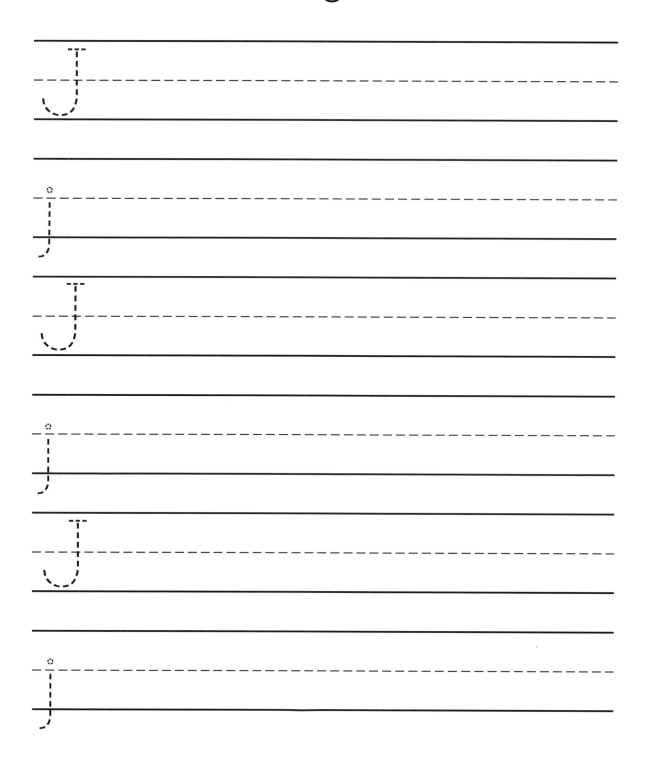

Practice writing the letter "J"

Trace the letter "K"

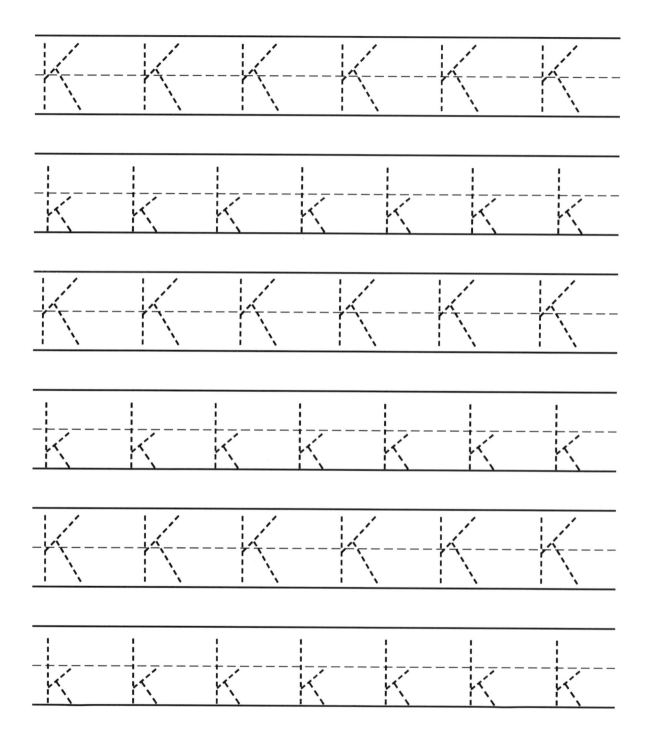

Trace the letter "K"

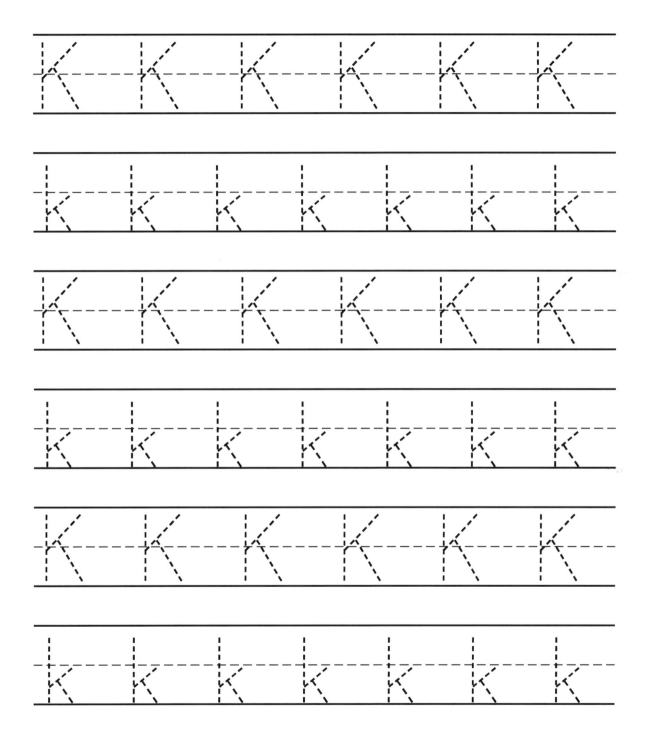

Practice writing the letter "K"

Practice writing the letter "K"

Trace the letter "L"

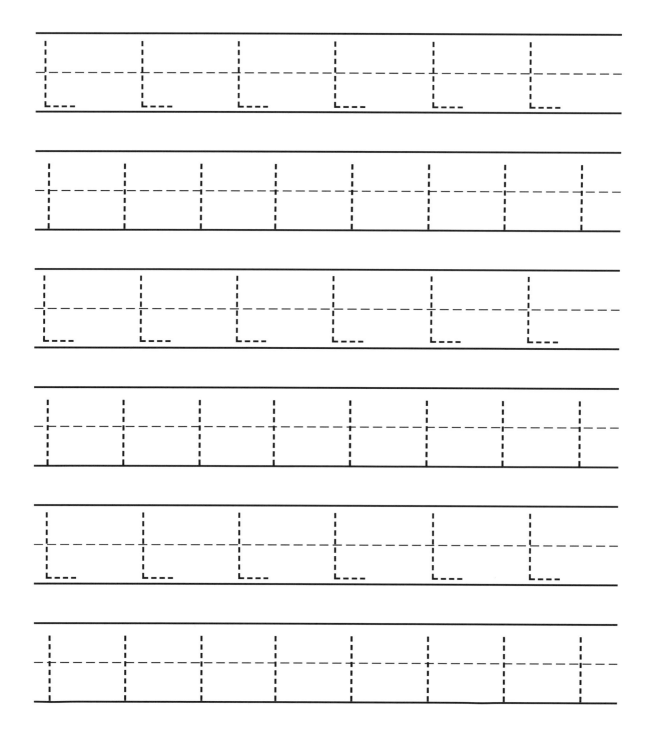

Trace the letter "L"

Practice writing the letter "L"

Practice writing the letter "L"

Trace the letter "M"

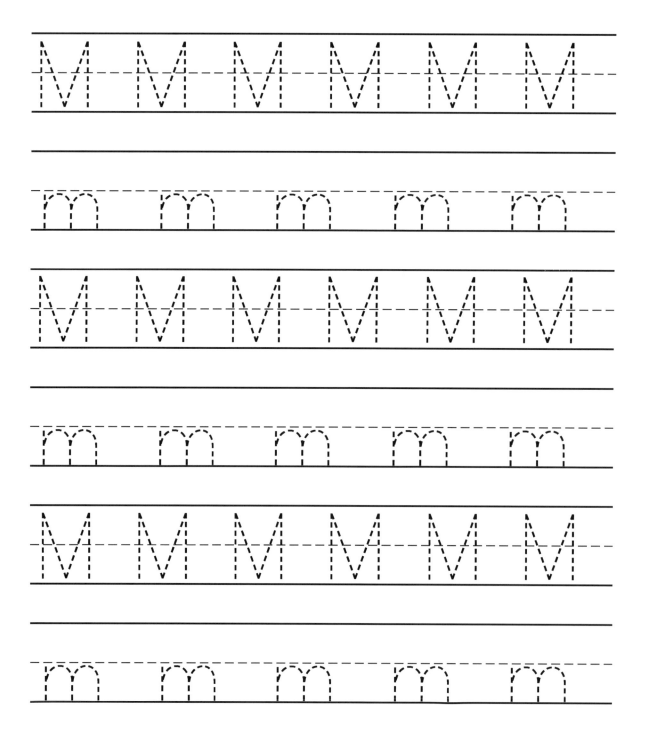

Trace the letter "M"

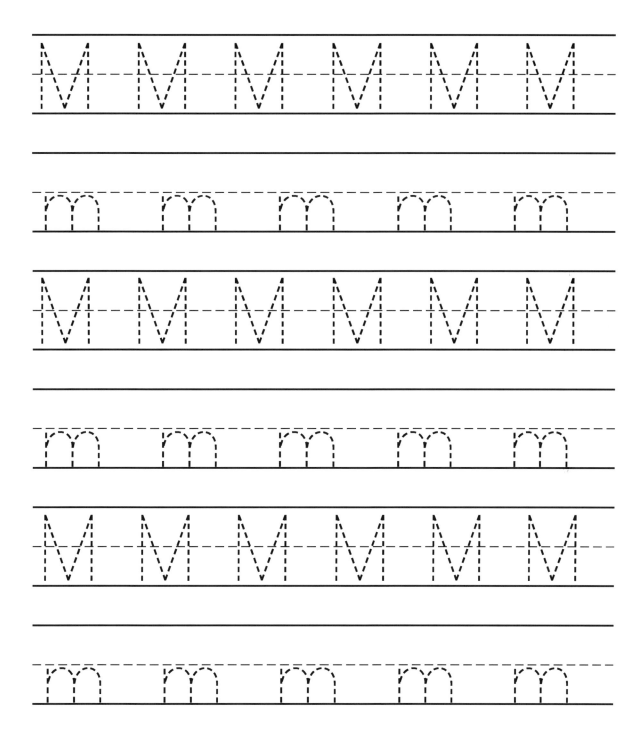

Practice writing the letter "M"

M _

m

M _

m _

M _

m _

Practice writing the letter "M"

M -

m -

M -

m -

M -

m -

Trace the letter "N"

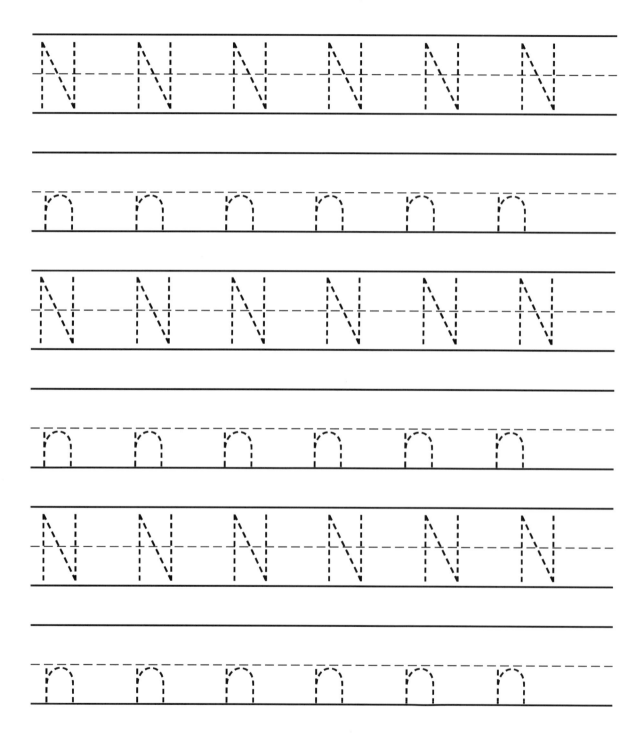

Trace the letter "N"

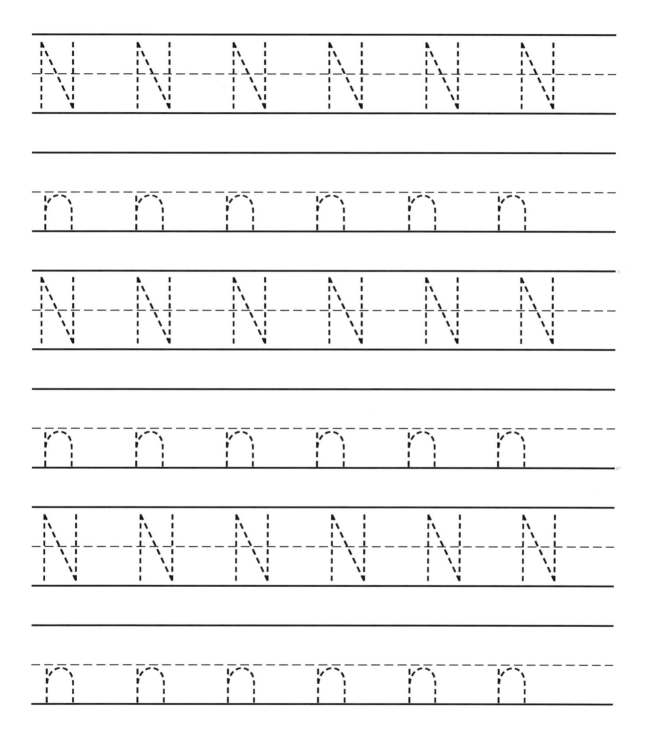

Practice writing the letter "N"

N

n

N

n

N

n

Practice writing the letter "N"

N

n

N

n

N

n

Trace the letter "O"

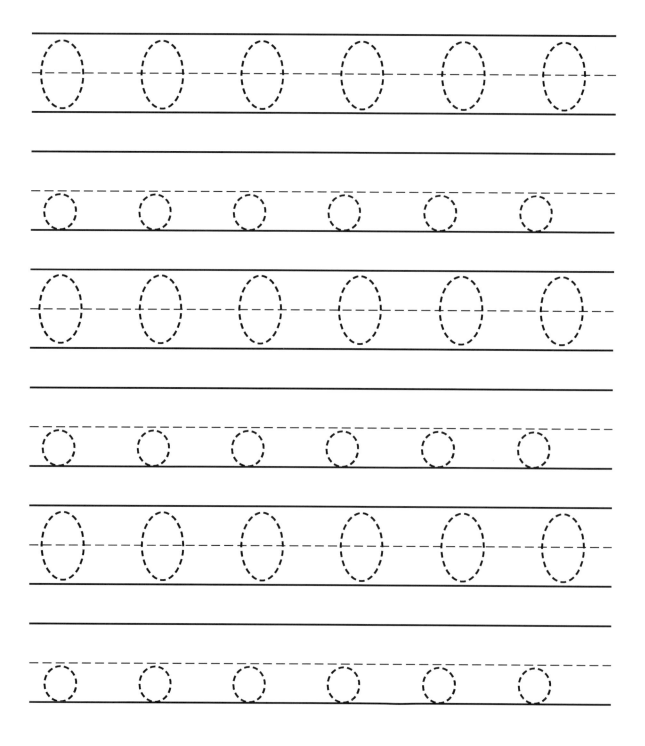

Trace the letter "O"

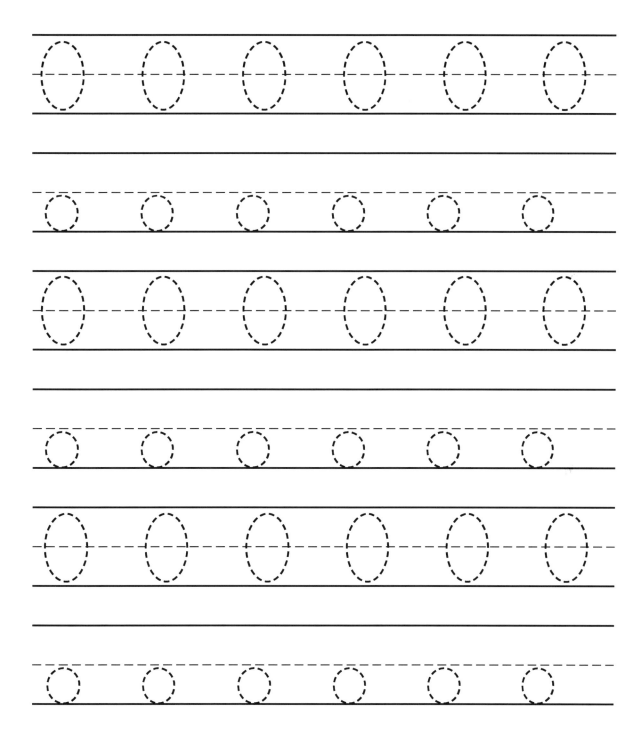

Practice writing the letter "O"

Practice writing the letter "O"

Trace the letter "P"

P P P P P

P P P P P P

P P P P P P

P P P P P P

P P P P P P

P P P P P P

Trace the letter "P"

P P P P P P

P P P P P P

P P P P P P

P P P P P P

P P P P P P

P P P P P P

Practice writing the letter "P"

P

P

P

P

P

P

Practice writing the letter "P"

Trace the letter "Q"

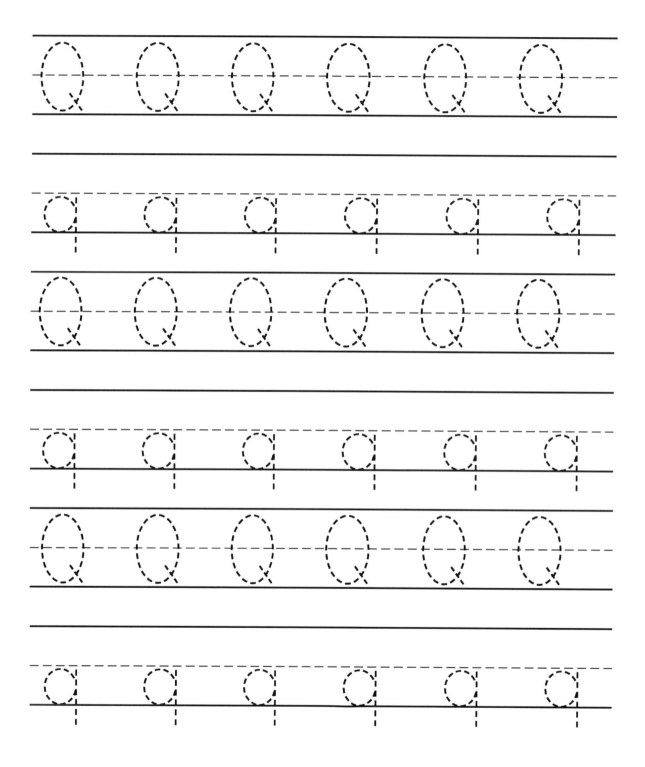

Trace the letter "Q"

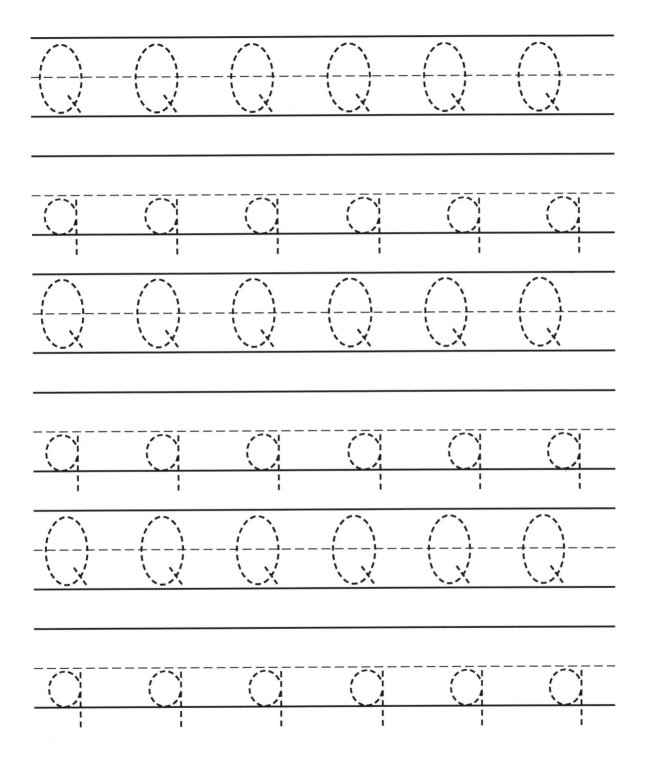

Practice writing the letter "Q"

Practice writing the letter "Q"

Trace the letter "R"

R R R R R

r r r r r r r

R R R R R

r r r r r r r

R R R R R

r r r r r r r

Trace the letter "R"

R R R R R

r r r r r r

R R R R R

r r r r r r

R R R R R

r r r r r r

Practice writing the letter "R"

R

r

R

r

R

r

Practice writing the letter "R"

R

r

R

r

R

r

Trace the letter "S"

S S S S S S

S S S S S S

S S S S S S

S S S S S S

S S S S S S

S S S S S S

Trace the letter "S"

S S S S S S

S S S S S S

S S S S S S

S S S S S S

S S S S S S

S S S S S S

Practice writing the letter "S"

S

S

S

S

S

S

Practice writing the letter "S"

S

S

S

S

S

S

Trace the letter "T"

Trace the letter "T"

Practice writing the letter "T"

Practice writing the letter "T"

Trace the letter "U"

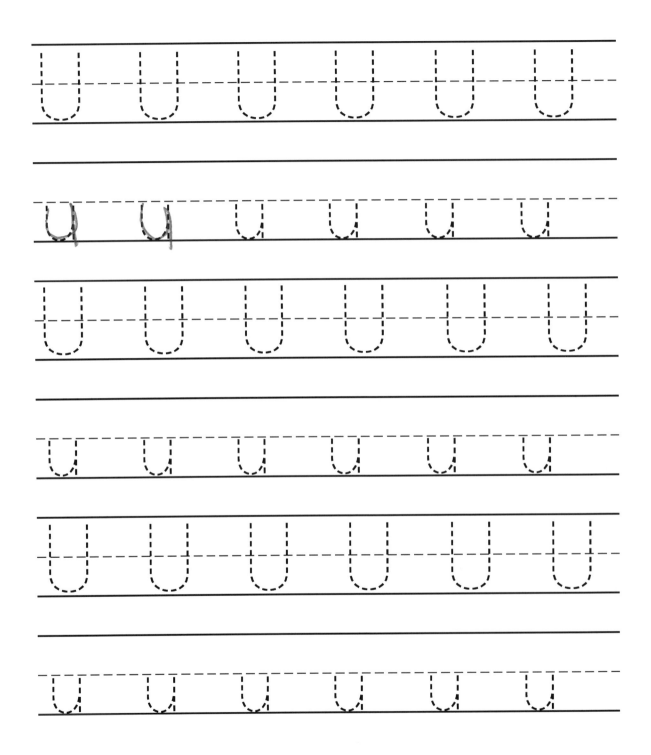

Trace the letter "U"

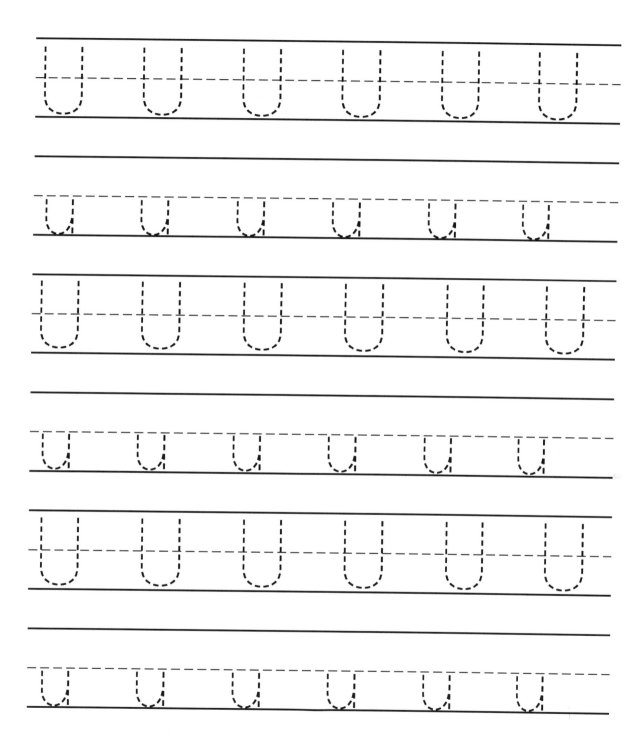

Practice writing the letter "U"

Practice writing the letter "U"

Trace the letter "V"

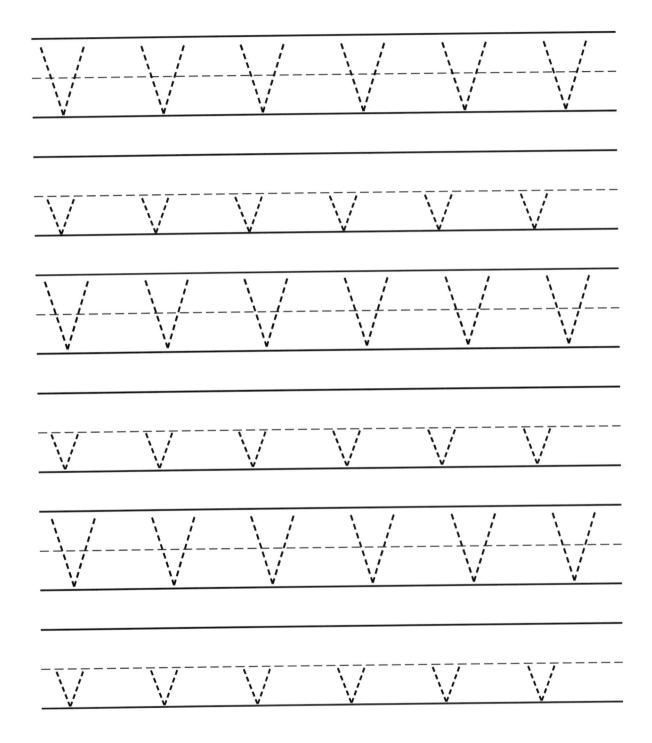

Trace the letter "V"

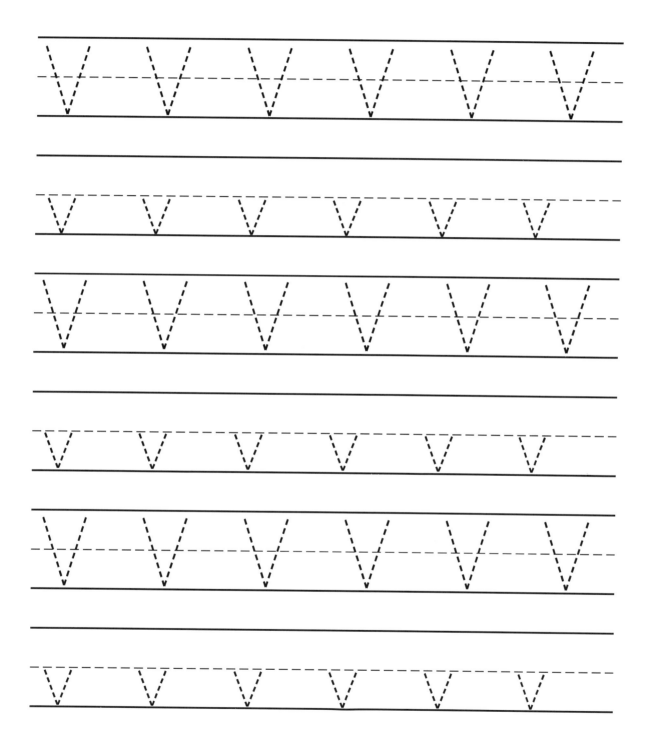

Practice writing the letter "V"

V

V

V

V

V

V

Practice writing the letter "V"

Trace the letter "W"

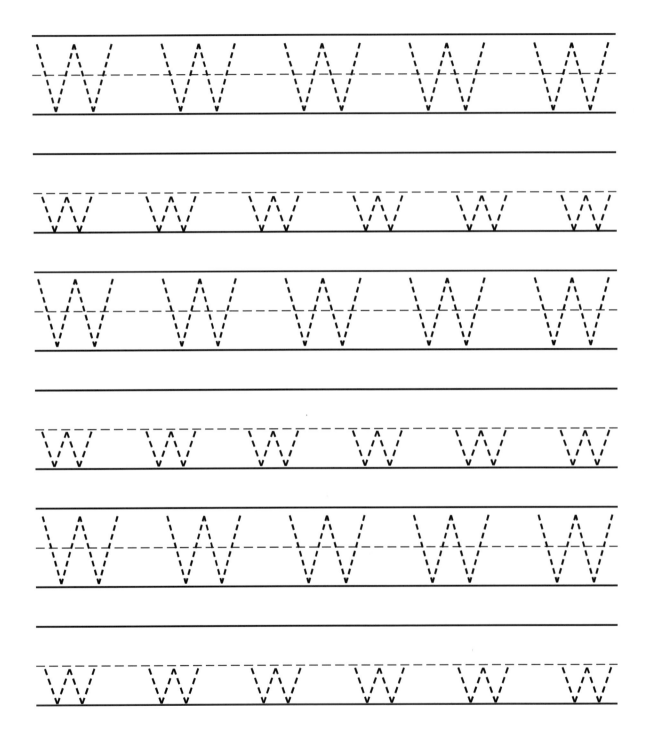

Trace the letter "W"

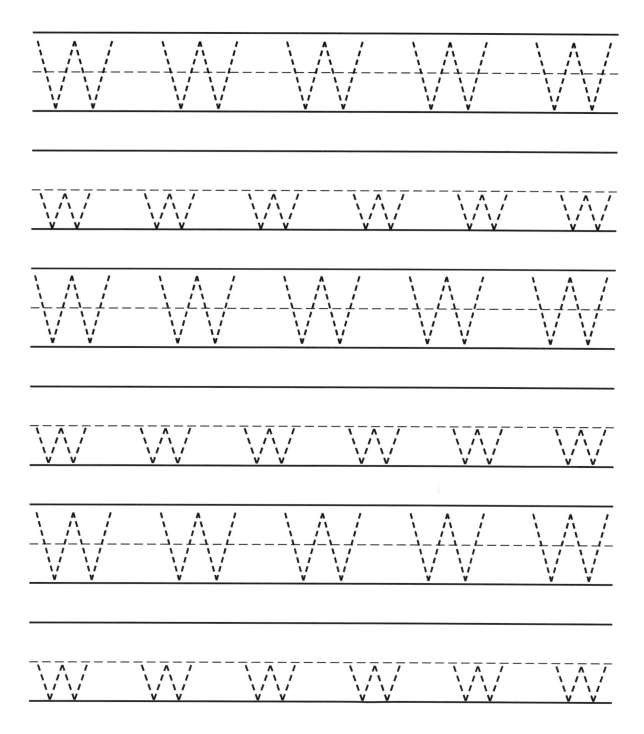

Practice writing the letter "W"

W

W

W

W

W

W

Practice writing the letter "W"

W

W

W

W

W

W

Trace the letter "X"

Trace the letter "X"

Practice writing the letter "X"

Practice writing the letter "X"

X
X
X
X
X
X

Trace the letter "Y"

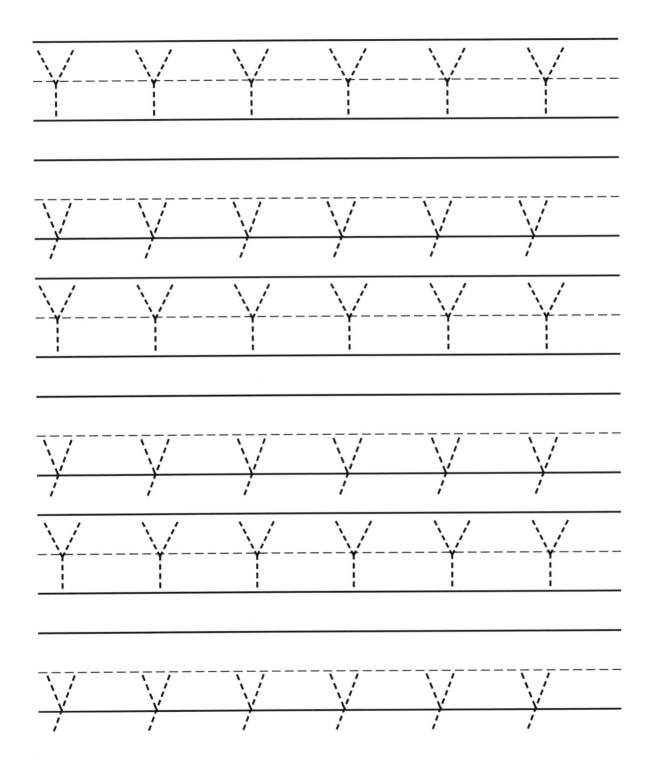

Trace the letter "Y"

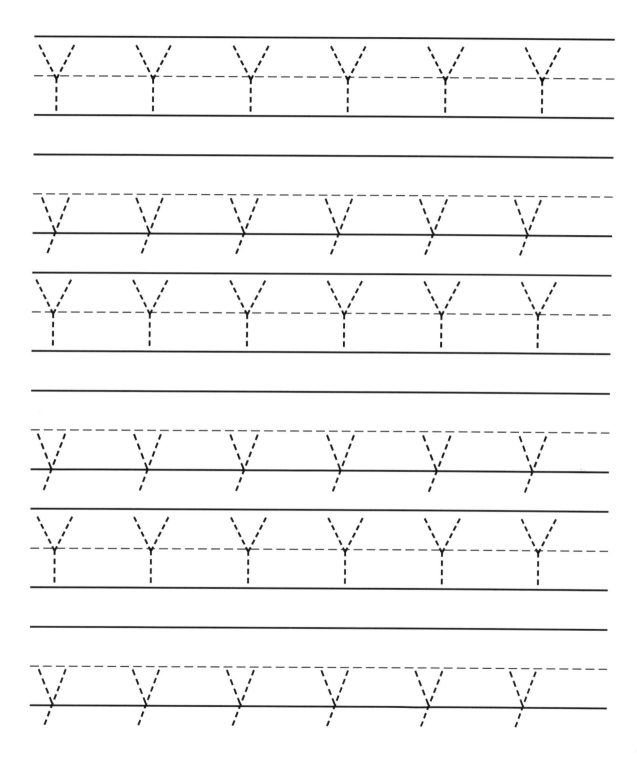

Practice writing the letter "Y"

Y

Y

Y

Y

Y

Y

Practice writing the letter "Y"

Trace the letter "Z"

Z Z Z Z Z Z

Z Z Z Z Z Z

Z Z Z Z Z Z

Z Z Z Z Z Z

Z Z Z Z Z Z

Z Z Z Z Z Z

Trace the letter "Z"

Practice writing the letter "Z"

Practice writing the letter "Z"

Z

Z

Z

Z

Z

Z

writing numbers 1-10

I can trace the number 1.

1 1 1 1 1 1 1 1

one one one

1 1 1 1 1 1 1

one one one

1 1 1 1 1 1 1

one one one

I can trace the number 1.

1 1 1 1 1 1 1

one one one

1 1 1 1 1 1 1

one one one

1 1 1 1 1 1 1

one one one

Practice writing the number 1.

1

one

1

one

1

one

Practice writing the number 1.

1 -

one -

1 -

one -

1 -

one -

I can trace the number 2.

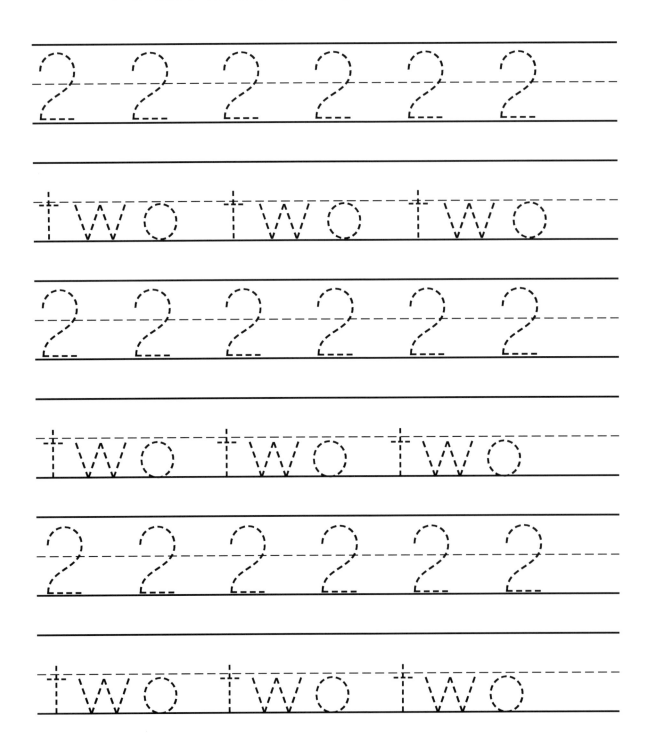

I can trace the number 2.

2 2 2 2 2 2

two two two

2 2 2 2 2 2

two two two

2 2 2 2 2 2

two two two

Practice writing the number 2.

2

two

2

two

2

two

Practice writing the number 2.

2

two

2

two

2

two

I can trace the number 3.

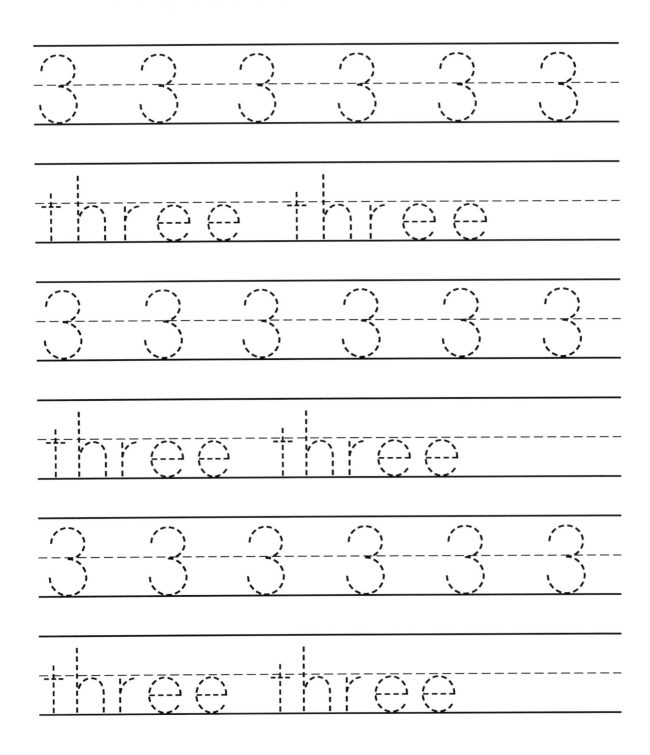

I can trace the number 3.

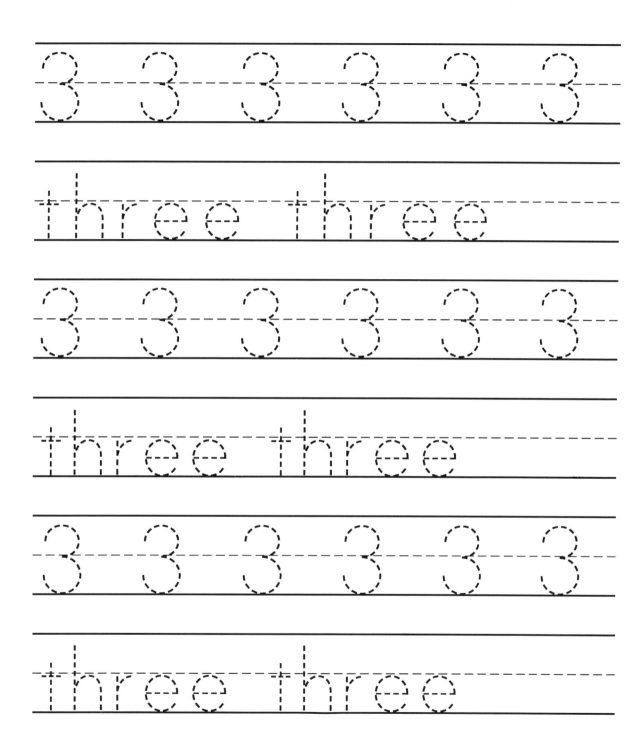

Practice writing the number 3.

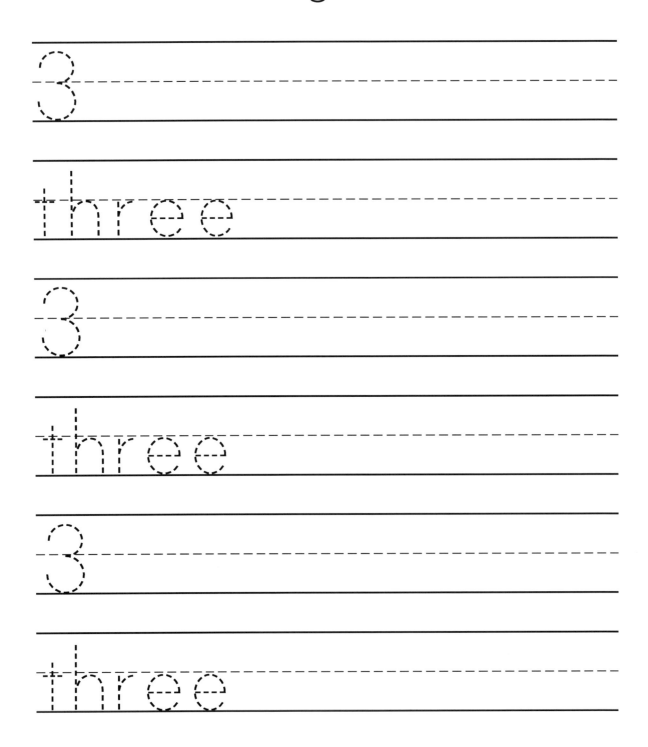

3

three

3

three

3

three

Practice writing the number 3.

3

three

3

three

3

three

I can trace the number 4.

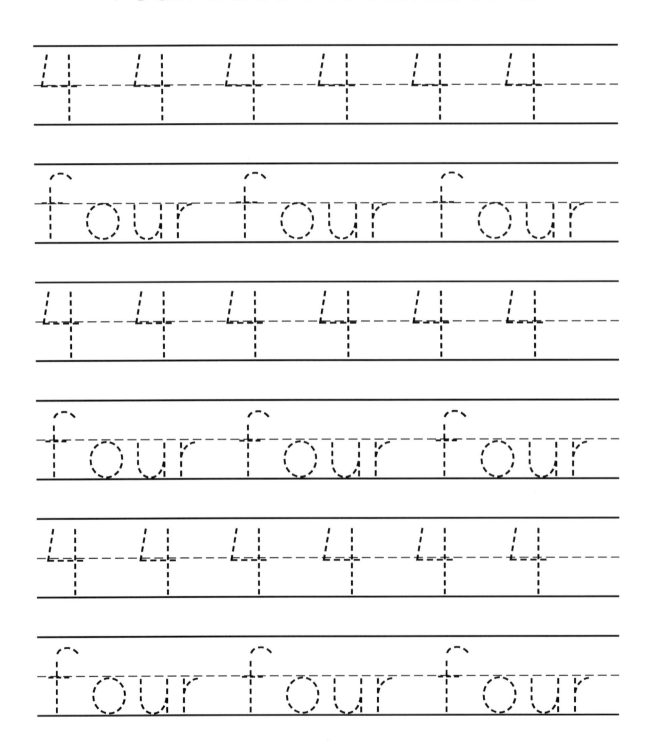

I can trace the number 4.

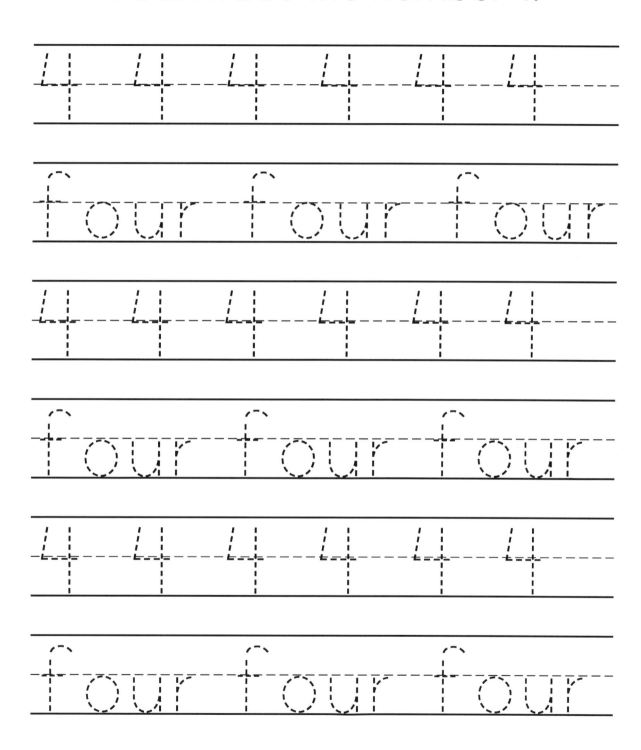

Practice writing the number 4.

4

four

4

four

4

four

Practice writing the number 4.

4

four

4

four

4

four

I can trace the number 5.

I can trace the number 5.

5 5 5 5 5 5

five five five

5 5 5 5 5 5

five five five

5 5 5 5 5 5

five five five

Practice writing the number 5.

Practice writing the number 5.

I can trace the number 6.

I can trace the number 6.

6　6　6　6　6　6

six　six　six　six

6　6　6　6　6　6

six　six　six　six

6　6　6　6　6　6

six　six　six　six

Practice writing the number 6.

6

six

6

six

6

six

Practice writing the number 6.

6 -

six -

6 -

six -

6 -

six -

I can trace the number 7.

7 7 7 7 7 7

seven   seven

7 7 7 7 7 7

seven   seven

7 7 7 7 7 7

seven   seven

I can trace the number 7.

7 7 7 7 7

seven   seven

7 7 7 7 7

seven   seven

7 7 7 7 7

seven   seven

Practice writing the number 7.

7

seven

7

seven

7

seven

Practice writing the number 7.

7

seven

7

seven

7

seven

I can trace the number 8.

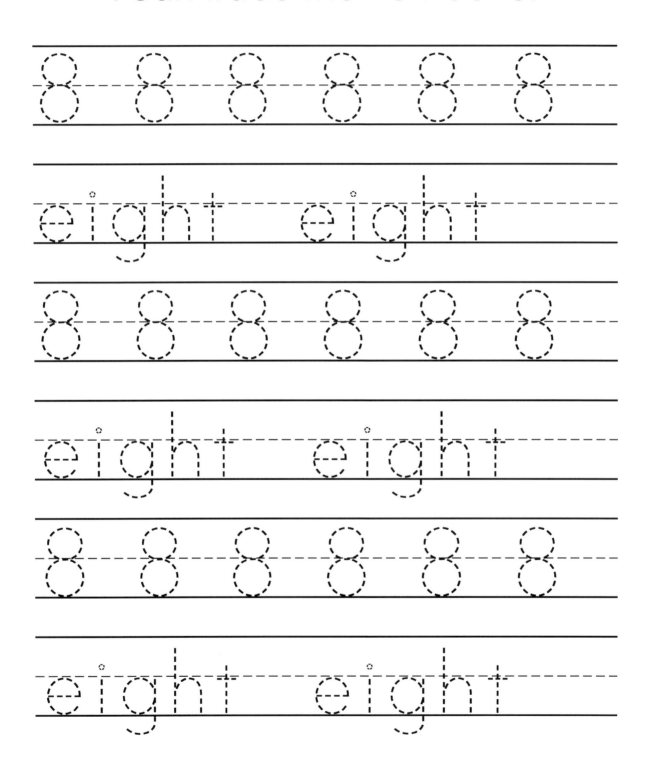

I can trace the number 8.

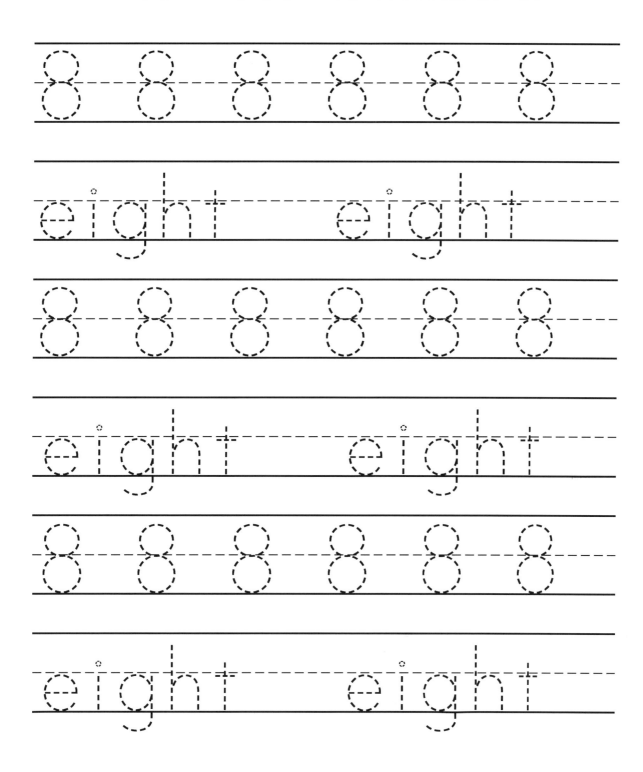

Practice writing the number 8.

Practice writing the number 8.

I can trace the number 9.

9 9 9 9 9 9

nine nine nine

9 9 9 9 9 9

nine nine nine

9 9 9 9 9 9

nine nine nine

I can trace the number 9.

9 9 9 9 9 9

nine nine nine

9 9 9 9 9 9

nine nine nine

9 9 9 9 9 9

nine nine nine

Practice writing the number 9.

9

nine

9

nine

9

nine

Practice writing the number 9.

9 -

nine -

9 -

nine -

9 -

nine -

I can trace the number 10.

10 10 10 10

ten ten ten ten

10 10 10 10

ten ten ten ten

10 10 10 10

ten ten ten ten

I can trace the number 10.

10 10 10 10 10

ten ten ten ten

10 10 10 10

ten ten ten ten

10 10 10 10

ten ten ten ten

Practice writing the number 10.

10

ten

10

ten

10

ten

Practice writing the number 10.

10

ten

10

ten

10

ten

Made in the USA
Lexington, KY
07 February 2018